STECK-VAUGHN

WORKFORCE: BUILDING SUCCESS

PERSONAL DEVELOPMENT

Project Consultant

Harriet Diamond
Diamond Associates
Westfield, NJ

Series Reviewers

Nancy Arnold
Metropolitan Adult
Education Program
San Jose, CA

Lou Winn Burns
Booker High School
Sarasota, FL

Jane Westbrook
Weatherford ISD
Community Services
Weatherford, TX

Ronald D. Froman
National Training &
Development Specialists
Winter Springs, FL

Dr. Randy Whitfield
North Carolina Community
College System
Raleigh, NC

Ann Jackson
Orange County
Public Schools
Orlando, FL

STECK-VAUGHN
ELEMENTARY · SECONDARY · ADULT · LIBRARY

A Harcourt Company

www.steck-vaughn.com

Acknowledgments

Steck-Vaughn Company
Executive Editor: Ellen Northcutt
Supervising Editor: Tim Collins
Senior Editor: Julie Higgins
Assistant Art Director: Richard Balsam
Design Manager: Danielle Szabo

Proof Positive/Farrowlyne Associates, Inc.
Program Editorial, Development, Design, and Production

Photo Credits
Cover Photo: © Michael Hart/FPG

Pp. 5, 6, 13, 15, 21, 23, 29, 30, 37, 38, 45, 47, 53, 55, 61, 63, 70, 71, 78, 79 © From: The ENTER HERE® Series, © 1995 by Enter Here L.L.C.; p. 4 © Michael Rosenfeld/Tony Stone Images; p. 12 © Charles Gupton/Tony Stone Images; p. 20 © Thomas Del Brase/Tony Stone Images; p. 28 © Michael Newman/PhotoEdit; p. 36 © Jon Riley/Tony Stone Images; p. 44 © Elena Rooraid/PhotoEdit; p. 52 © David Young-Wolff/PhotoEdit; p. 60 © Lawrence Manning/Tony Stone Images; p. 68 © Michael Newman/PhotoEdit; p. 76 © Super Stock International.

ISBN 0-8172-6519-8

Contents

To the Learner

Workforce: Building Success is a series of six books designed to help you improve key job skills. You will find many ways to improve, whether you're working or preparing to find a job. This book, *Personal Development*, is about ways to monitor and improve your work performance. To develop your career, you need to act responsibly and do quality work.

Before you begin the lessons, take the Check What You Know skills inventory, check your answers, and fill out the Preview Chart. There you will see which skills you already know and which you need to practice.

After you finish the last practice page, take the Check What You've Learned inventory, check your answers, and fill out the Review Chart. You'll see what great progress you've made.

Each lesson is followed by four types of exercises:

- The questions in **Comprehension Check** will help you make sure you understood the reading.
- In **Making Connections,** you will read about situations in which people need to use the skills in the reading.
- In the next section, called **Try It Out, Act It Out,** or **Talk It Out,** you will complete an activity that requires you to use the new skills. You might interview someone, conduct a survey, make a telephone call, have a discussion, or role play a situation.
- In **Think and Apply,** you will think about how well you use the skills in your daily life. Then you will decide which skills you want to improve and make a plan to reach your goal.

At the end of the book, you will find a Glossary and an Answer Key. Use the Glossary to look up definitions of key work-related words. Use the Answer Key to check your answers to many of the exercises.

Check What You Know will help you know how well you understand personal development skills. It will also show you which skills you need to improve.

Read each question. Circle the letter before the answer.

1. Nick wants to review his performance in his new job. It would be best for him to

   a. be honest and accurate.

   b. ignore others' feedback.

   c. give himself high marks to keep his confidence up.

2. Jeff, Mack, and Hanna work for a mailing house. Which person does work without being asked?

   a. Jeff always does the work he is assigned by his supervisor.

   b. Mack fills the time by reading the sports pages when work is slow.

   c. Hanna has proposed a new, more efficient way to organize the mailings.

3. Building a group of coworkers that will support you

   a. is a last resort if you cannot carry out your tasks.

   b. can be an important way of helping you on the job.

   c. means they cannot rely on you for advice.

4. Susie has been putting off writing a report because she is afraid she won't do well. How could Susie overcome this fear?

   a. She should not think of success and failure as "all or nothing."

   b. She should insist that her report be perfect.

   c. She should get it over with as quickly as possible.

5. Maya needs someone who can help her with a rush job with many tasks. Which of the following employees would be best for this job?

   a. Jim likes to focus on doing one thing at a time.

   b. Jerry does not like to ask others for help.

   c. Bill works best when he is under pressure.

6. Which of the following is not a responsible attitude toward work?

   a. being on time for a meeting
   b. keeping it to yourself when you cannot complete your tasks
   c. calling in ahead of time when you are sick

7. Ben is working to develop a positive self-image at his job. What method will help him to do this?

   a. He should put any thought of his own weaknesses out of his mind.
   b. He should not accept any compliments until he has completed his own self-evaluation.
   c. He should identify his strengths and weaknesses, and use his strengths to overcome his weaknesses.

8. Vince works in the shipping department of a meat supply company. He would like to be promoted and work in the office. Which is not a good way for him to work for this promotion?

   a. He should learn more about the industry.
   b. He should ask his supervisor about job opportunities.
   c. He should consult his supervisor whenever possible.

9. Dennis is starting a new job on an assembly line. Each person is trained to work on all parts of the line. New employees are trained by a coworker. Which of the following is true about the workers on this line?

   a. There is a great deal of emphasis on teamwork.
   b. Communicating well is not important.
   c. Since there is more teamwork, the individual is not responsible for his or her work.

2